The 9 C.L.E.A.R. V.I.E.W. ™ Tips
To Powerful Life Transformations

9 Simple Steps for achieving powerful life transformations and have your best life NOW!!

By Tabitha L. McClarity

Copyright

The 9 C.L.E.A.R. V.I.E.W. ™ Tips to Powerful Life Transformations: 9 Simple Steps for achieving powerful life transformations and have your best life NOW!!

Copyright © 2012 by Tabitha McClarity

All rights reserved. No part of this book may be reproduced or transmitted in any forms or by any means, electronic or mechanical, including photocopying or recording or by any information storage or retrieval system without written permission of Tabitha L. Rowland McClarity, except for the inclusions of brief quotations in a review.

The purpose of this book is to educate and entertain. The author and/or publisher do not guarantee that anyone following these techniques, suggestions, tips, ideas, or strategies will become successful. The author and/or publisher shall have neither liability nor responsibility to anyone with respect to any loss or damage caused, or alleged to be caused, directly or indirectly by the information contained in this book.

ISBN 13:   978-0615745015

ISBN 10:   0615745016

Please look for these Titles by Tabitha L. McClarity

I Forgive Me: 31 days of Self Forgiveness:
In order to be able to TRULY forgive others I have to forgive me first!!!

Empowerment...My Power...ME:
5 Steps to creating Self Encouragement, Self Respect and Self Power

ITeam: I Don't Care What Anyone Says...There is an "I" in Team!!!

No Money Mo Problems: 6 Steps to Reduce Debt and Live With the Money You Make

R-E-S-P-E-C-T the Money and it will stay with you longer

Three Tenths Money Strategy: Savings, Tithing and Investing my way Financial Freedom

Lord I want to be made whole: Spiritually, Mentally, Physically & Financially; The four stages to experience true Wholeness (four book series)

For more information about this Author, Speaker, Life/Success Coach visit us on the web ***www.tabithamcclarity.com***

Contents

Acknowledgement ii

Preface iii

Introduction vii

Tip #1 – Commitment 1

Tip #2 – Learn 4

Tip #3 – Energize 10

Tip #4 – Articulate 14

Tip #5 – Realize 17

Tip #6 – Visualize 20

Tip #7 – Initiate 23

Tip #8 – Evaluate 27

Tips #9 – WIN! 30

Now that you have a C.L.E.A.R. V.I.E.W. ™ 32

Acknowledgement

To God, Thank you for giving the awe inspiring word to transform the lives of your people. To help them to live the life you said we could have right now. Thank you for opening my heart, my eyes, my mouth and my mind. Oh that you are Glorified!! To Randy, Husband and best friend, I love you, thank you for helping me to stay encouraged and believing in my dreams. To My Children & Grandchildren, Chris, Shay, Deana, DeVonte, Quindarious, D'Aja, Peyton & Azala—you are my focus; I love you! To my parents Jerry & Ruby Rowland...I am so blessed to have you as my main role models...I love you. To my Siblings Carmen, Jerry, Melissa, Tara, Sterling, Micah & Courtney, you mean the world to me, I love you!!! To all my nieces & nephews...Auntie Lynne Loves you, don't stop chasing your dreams. To all of my cousins, we grew up like sisters and brothers, I would not change our lives for anything Niecie, Carla, Delia, Tonia, Shell, India, Tedra, Lisa & Judy, thank you for allowing me to be in your presence all these years!! To my girls, Latanja, Reecie, Torrie, Anita, and Karessa, Lord, the conversations that we have had...Thank you for being my friends. I love you guys!! To my Pastor & Wife, Ramon & Tijuana Arnold—Thank you for always having my back, for your words, guidance & encouragement; I appreciate you guys so much, I love you!!

Preface

Thank you so much for purchasing this book!! It was born out of the heart of my wanting to see your life transformed in a POWERFUL way. As I began to create my website I created The 9 C.L.E.A.R. V.I.E.W. ™ Tips as a way to get you to stop looking behind you in the rear view of what was and to focus on what is now and what lies ahead. Don't get me wrong understanding yesterday helps to shape your values and helps you not to do some of the same negative things but looking behind you also clouds your view and sometimes causes you to miss the awesome blessings and opportunities you have right in front of you. See let me tell you a little story.

Some years ago the city I lived in was hit by a moderate snow storm, it has snowed in our neighborhood and there was a blanket of snow all over my SUV. Well in attempts to surprise me by getting the snow off of my car, my sons scraped the snow off my car and wiped as much of the ice they could off the door mirrors. While trying to get the remaining ice off of my mirrors, they poured hot water on my door mirrors to melt the snow away. Well as science would have it, the cold ice and hot water mixture caused my mirror to shatter. The mirror did not break out it was just shattered in place. I was initially angry but got over it because their intentions were to help me. Anyway I have never gotten that mirror fixed and drive the vehicle with a shattered mirror still to this day. One day I was using that mirror to drive (as I have for the last eight or nine years). This particular day I had been thinking about the past and how it controls so many people's lives, how they are not able to have their best life because of fear or because of repeating past mistakes. As I sat in traffic looking at one shattered door mirror then glancing at the center rear view mirror and then to the left door rear view mirror I made a connection to how the past is very similar to a rear view mirror. Out of my driver's side "rear view" mirror, I could see a reflection of everything on my left except for the things that were in my blind spots, out of my center rear view mirror I could clearly see what was directly behind me and out of the passenger door rear view mirror I could see everything that was on the right side except for what was in my blind spot. I want to focus a little bit more on the passenger side review mirror. See in my SUV, this particular mirror had been broken. I had learned to focus on one part of the broken mirror and use it as my mirror to make decisions with, I made decisions on whether I would change lanes or not, if I could see if anyone was coming up on my right side, whether or not I could back up safely etc. and for the last eight or nine years I have been able to do this without an issue, not because of the one mirror alone, but because I used all the mirrors together. However, even with using the other mirrors, I still had blind spots and things that I could not see. What has really helped me avoid an accident over the years is that I used the entire view that I have (mostly looking in front of me) to make decisions for passing, merging and backing up. Life is the same way. There are things in our past that has broken us and causes us not to see and/or comprehend what is in front of us. A lot of us have gotten stuck in a backwards mentality and it affects the life that we could have now. How many times have you said...I tried that before, it did not work then, and it is not going to work now? Or I know someone who did that a few years ago it did not work so I am not going to try it. Well this book is created to challenge that fear and doubt and help you to experience the blessing and joy you are destined to have. Your Powerful Transformation does not have to be massive it could be something that is *small, but it has a strong connection to you. That is what you want to apply these tips to. Is this a get rich quick book? NOPE. Is it a book that promises joy and happiness? NOPE. But it is a book that will help you envision your life differently and take steps to make powerful transformations towards a positive future. So before you read another page………TAKE A DEEP BREATH…….*

Tabula Rasa

Introduction

Are you ready to start living the best life you can have right now? Tabula Rasa means "blank slate". I want you to read this book with an open mind. Be willing to wipe the slate clean and start from scratch. Look for ways to have a C.L.E.A.R. V.I.E.W. ™ in your life.

In a few more pages you will be given 9 tips to help you achieve clarity and view life's conquerable challenges in a different way. Most like any other transformation in your life the tips will not work if you do not do them, if you do not want to do them and if you do not want to see a transformation in your life.

For many years I have had people ask me how I handle life's challenges, and why do I always seem happy, how do I accomplish my successes well here it is. I've used this process time and time again and been able to consistently release negativity, create positive transformation, operate with a more forward looking/forward living attitude, and achieve self defined success in my goals. You can do it too. I am so excited for you!!!

This is what I call a mini-book. It is not difficult reading, but the key is meditating on what you have read and then putting what you have read into action. In reality it should take you nine weeks to read this book and to put the tips into action. Minimize the other activities you are doing and do not try to apply the C.L.E.A.R. V.I.E.W. ™ Tips all at once or to several things at once. Take your time. You have spent quite some time (possibly years) looking in the rear view and making your decisions solely on negativity and the past. It is a process shift to focus on having a clear view and making decisions to live your life in the present moment.

C- Commitment

L- Learn

E-Energize

A-Articulate

R-Realize

V-Visualize

I-Initiate

E-Evaluate

W-WIN!

9 C.L.E.A.R. V.I.E.W™ Tips to Powerful Transformation

Tip #1 – Commitment

*Tip #1: The first tip for getting a **C.L.E.A.R. V.I.E.W.** ™ is to make the __commitment__ to actions that will allow you to create your Powerful transformation.*

Any change, upgrade, transition or transformation that is made requires a made up mind in order to come to past. You just cannot say "I want to change or I want to become better" and not dedicate yourself thoughts and efforts to make the change.

Being committed means that you in a state of being dedicated to a cause, activity, life style, decision etc. A commitment is NEVER suppose to be broken.

Isn't that a strong definition? When I started typing it I began to feel a little shame because I thought of all the things I started and did not finish because I was not committed to them. I wasn't committed because the things on my list were not as important as other priorities I thought I had. I always put other people and other things before me and things that were good for me. Does that sound familiar? We all do it.

Today is a call to action for you. I am calling you to stop and take a moment to focus on one or two immediate transformations you want to have. Then write them down. I want you to look at the words and make a commitment (a promise) to yourself to see the transformation all the way through. Before you are able to move forward you have to be committed to the change that you want to happen in your life. Without commitment you cannot accomplish the task. Why? because just as soon as you decide what your Powerful transformation is; whether it is reconnecting with your spouse, losing weight, starting a business, recommitting to your faith, increasing your self esteem, establishing or reestablishing your relationship with your children, going to school, writing a book etc. ALL HELL is going to break loose. Negativity and self doubt will creep in and because you don't want to be uncomfortable you will give in and maintain the status quo. NOT TODAY. You have to decide today to dedicate some time and some effort to create the Powerful transformation you want.

This week take the following steps to establish a commitment to the Powerful transformation you want.

1. Say I am committed to making the effort to _____ (fill in the blank)
2. Get a note book to record your progress
3. Be careful about sharing transformation with anyone (Sometimes people have a way of killing our dreams)
4. Take time to meditate on what commitment means and how you will remain committed to your desired transformation.
5. Acknowledge that you are important and that your transformation is here to allow you have your best life now.

These 9 Tips are about you, about you becoming stronger, about you becoming more powerful, about you reconnecting with yourself and your dreams. It is about being present and not just going through the motions of living. It is about tapping into your gifts and into your destiny. It is about taking time to clear the clutter that you have picked up as you navigated *this maze we call life. It is a bout connecting with your purpose. Will you dedicate yourself to that?*

I invite you to come on this journey. Make a promise to yourself and become dedicated to a new cause; to a YOU cause. Resolve not to break this commitment to yourself. If you do not declare your commitment today, and I mean RIGHT NOW, then the remainder of these wonderful tips will do you no good.

Dedicate yourself to a new cause; to a YOU cause.

Tip #2 – Learn

*Tip #2: The second tip for getting a C.L.E.A.R. V.I.E.W. ™ is to **learn** or research information to achieve your Powerful transformation.*

Life is continually changing. No matter where you work, who your friends are or how much money you make; you will always have to learn something. One of my favorite Bible verses says, "Wisdom is the principal (main) thing, therefore get wisdom: and with all thy getting, get understanding (be a continuous learner,)" Proverbs 4:7. Getting an understanding requires us to read and comprehend what we read. Once we have a level of comprehension then the information is learned. This can be done through reading, seeing the task or doing a task.

For this tip take the transformations that you want to achieve and write down what you know about the subject. If you find that you do not know much, research and learn what you need to know.

For example: If your transformation is to learn a new language then one of the things you would write would be "What is the process of learning this new language?" The answer would be Finding a class or finding the software to teach me the language. In answering that one question you have learned about two ways to have the Powerful transformation of leaning a new language.

Maybe the powerful transformation you want is to own a business. One of the questions you would write would be "What type of business do I want to own?" Once you have decided that the next question could be "How much do I know about running X type of business?" If you did not know anything then you would use the means of talking to others in the business that you want to be in, researching on the internet, reading books about the business so on and so forth. After some time in doing your research you will have learned something about the transformation that you want to make.

My friend this step is very critical DO NOT go by what you think you know about your transformation; don't even go by what someone told you last time. Start fresh and start new. I guarantee you will find new and rewarding information to usher you into your Powerful transformation.

In the introduction, I told you that it would take you nine weeks to read and apply these tips to your life to achieve the Powerful Transformation that you are planning to achieve but I really want you to take your time with the learning tip. I know you have heard the phrase "I had to learn from the School of Hard Knocks" well this is one of those times and you want to take in consideration what I am trying to teach you. I mean after all, there is a reason why you are reading these Tips. It is because you want a POWERFUL TRANSFORMATION in your life and the things you have been trying are just not working for you. So it is time to learn something new. When you take your time to truly learn something you increase your chances of being successful at it.

If your transformation is going to cause you to have to learn a lot of information, I urge you to break it up in stages. For example: Starting a business. There is the stage where you decide you want to open a business, there is the stage where you research the market in your area, there is the stage where you look for the location, there is the stage where you plan the finances, there is the stage where you plan your brand…etc. I could name about 10 more things that would take time for you to learn but I am assuming you get the picture about learning. Take it in small chunks, believe me, learning about your Powerful transformation is the key to making it a manifestation!!!

What I love about learning is that through getting the right understanding you are able to make informed decisions about the choices you want to make!!

We are moving on to tip # 3. Over the next week ponder these questions and take action in changing some of your learning habits.

- How often do you pick up a book?

    Aim to read one per month

- How often do you read the news paper?

    Aim to read at least once per week

- How often do you update your short and long term goals (Personal & Professional)?

If you have never had short term or long term goals start.Creating these goals could actually be a Powerful Transformation...i.e. "The Powerful Transformation I want to make is to create a Personal goals Plan" then start listing what all would go in that plan and prioritize what you want to transform first. You could possibly do a few things on the list but DO NOT over do it. Remember you want to succeed.

- *How often do you attend Conferences and Seminars to invest in your growth?*

    You should invest in yourself by attending conferences and seminars. Some of them cost so you should budget to attend. You goal should be to do this at least once per year

- *Do you have a mentor?*

    Not your friends, but someone who is objective and can help you stay grounded and focused on you what you are trying to accomplish. Who can teach you?

Proverbs 4:7

"Wisdom is the principal thing, therefore get wisdom: and with all thy getting, get understanding."

Tip #3 – Energize

Tip #3: The third tip for getting a C.L.*E*.A.R. V.I.E.W. ™ is to **energize** yourself. Do not wait on someone else to hype you up. You want this Powerful transformation and only you can make it come to pass, embrace the empowered you!!

When I got to this tip I and read the definition of energize, I could not help but to smile. WOW...get this; energize means to give vitality and enthusiasm to...Are you ready?

Now that you have made the commitment to achieving the transformation that you want and you have begin to learn about yourself and what it truly means to have your Powerful transformation...you cannot just sit there and twiddle your thumbs...IT IS TIME TO WORK!!!

Start the energy moving through your body, through your mind and through your spirit. Encourage yourself to press toward your goals!!

1. Make a conscious choice to think positively about your life and about your transformation EVERYDAY
2. Don't wait on someone to encourage you, encourage yourself
3. Make healthy Food choices eat food that will give you vitality and physical energy to support your mental and spiritual energy
4. Surround yourself with positive energetic people
5. SMILE

If the Powerful Transformation you want to make is to lose weight then guess what? You have to do something to make that weight come off. It may be walking 20 minutes a day then upping that to 30 minutes and so on and so forth. YOU have to do something. You have to motivate yourself even when you do not want to go!!

Maybe the Powerful transformation you want is to own your own house, well you cannot just sit there. The first thing you need to do is decide where you want to live and go look! You guessed it; again YOU HAVE TO DO SOMETHING. Be excited about the new opportunity of being a home owner.

People who know me know that I LOVE LOVE LOVE wrestling, I am talking about the professional wrestling where the wrestlers jump from tables and off of the top of ropes Etc. I think one of the things that I love about it is because it is so alive and the wrestlers are electrifying. Imagine this...there is a small eight by eight ring in the middle of an arena that could house thousands and thousands of people. All of these people came to see you perform, to see you wrestle, to see you bring some action into their lives...what type of match would it be if the you nonchalantly moseyed down the platform and took your time to get in the ring, there was no trash talking or hyper sidekick running around the ring...just a lackadaisical wrestler waiting on your opponent....THAT would be a travesty!!! NO ONE would want to see that. We want to see John Cena running to the ring and doing his introductory hand wave..."YOU CAN'T SEE ME!!" We want to see the famed Rey Mysterio do a high flying dive from the top rope...we even want to hear a "WHHEEWW brother " from Rick Flare...Why because for wrestling fans it is the ENERGY...IT ENERGIZES us to be a part of the show! Well guess what you have to do have that same energy for your POWERFUL TRANSFORMATION. There is someone in the audience of your life that you give energy to...it could be your spouse, your children, your co-worker or even yourself, but when you allow life to take that energy away it deflates all the positive energy that surrounds you. Before long you don't want to go to the park, you don't want to go have a date night with your spouse or a hang out night with your friends. You take your tired lifeless self home and wonder why life is not fulfilling anymore. Every day is show time every minute that you have is a blessing. You have to consistently speak vitality and enthusiasm into your life. So right now in your note book...I ask what the powerful transformation you want to make is. How are you energizing yourself to make it happen? WRITE IT DOWN and meditate on it...See you next week.

Focus everyday on increasing your mental and physical energy....Energize yourself...Stir up your gift :>)

Energize yourself Stir up your gift

:>)

Tip #4 – Articulate

Tip #4: The forth tip for getting a C.L.E.A.R. V.I.E.W. ™ is to articulate your Powerful transformation and repeat it over and over again. Speak it into existence.

By definition the word articulate means to express an idea or feeling fluently and coherently. Simply put...SAY IT and Say it in a way that is clear and understandable to you and anyone else who will be used as an instrument to usher you into your POWERFUL Transformation

I remember when my children were young and they began to talk, if they wanted something from the kitchen they would go to the refrigerator and point or go to the pantry and point, after a few rounds of charades, I figured out what they were talking about and could get the item for them. As I began to teach them to speak I remember saying "Say Mama, Say water, Say baba" so on and so forth. As they started learning to use their voice they would walk to the area and now would say I want water, I want juice, I want apple. They learned to articulate what they wanted. It that is a simple example, but guess what we use very similar language skills today. In your mind right now, you may know the Powerful transformation you want and need, but it has always only been in your mind. You have been pointing to it, daydreaming about it; you may have even expressed it a little to someone else. However if you do not know how to clearly articulate about the transformation, then how can you clearly make it come alive?

I have had many people start to tell me about their dreams and for whatever reason they lose the words and would say, "You know what I mean?" Sometimes I did sometime I didn't. Even when I was able to help them formulate what they wanted to say; the words were my words not theirs.

Your words and your transformation have meaning to you. You need to be able to say what you want. I dare you to try it right now. I know you have written it down because I have told you to do that a few times in the previous tips so now I am telling you to say what your Powerful Transformation is. Use these three steps to articulate your Powerful Transformation.

1. Select the words that really say what you want

2. Say what you want out loud. SAY IT CLEARLY and SAY IT LOUD!

   MY POWERFUL TRANSFORMATION IS TO

   _____

3. Practice repeating what your powerful transformation so that it will take root in your spirit.

Now that you have that off your chest how did you feel? Did your husband/wife say Huh? Maybe they asked you "Who are you talking to?" Give them a copy of the tips in a few weeks you will hear them talking to themselves also…Hahaha

Over the next week, articulate your transformation, say it when you get up, say it when you are in your car, if you feel comfortable, and share it with your family and friends. It's your life, and you have the right to transform it to whatever you want it to be. Live your purpose. See you next week

"My powerful Transformation is to _____"

(Say what you want)

Tip #5 – Realize

Tip #5: The fifth tip for getting a C.L.E.A.R. V.I.E.W. ™ is to realize that your powerful transformation obtainable. Your transformation is now a fact, it is real and you understand how to make it manifest.

When something is real we can see it, touch, feel it and taste it if we wanted to. Your Powerful transformation is the same way. Realizing that your transformation is in your grasp is an awesome feeling. When you realize your transformation you still have not hit the "go button" yet, but you are almost there. The realization stage is so critical because this is where you start to get the butterflies in your stomach. You may even start second guessing yourself, but just remember you are on the edge of something magnificent. You are at a place that you have never been before. Take a deep breath, go back to your note book and review all the steps you have taken to make this transformation. You got here because you believed in yourself, you believe in your dreams; you believe in the newness that you want to create for yourself. You have done the work and have the knowledge to move forward.

This powerful transformation is just for you.

Realization is sitting in the moment and saying, I am really about to go to college

OR

Wow, I am really about to take these flying lessons

OR

I am really about to open this business

OR

I am really about to _____ (you fill in the blanks)

Right now your Powerful transformation is your fact and you should be relieved that you are at this point of the transformation. Many people make it here, but they turn back. You cannot turn around now!! Your Powerful Transformation is concrete existent, it is real and you can have it.

A realized transformation has the following characteristics:

1. *You "know" it can be done*
2. *You have more confidence about how to achieve the transformation*
3. *You are excited to make the transformation*
4. *You start to "see" the transformation come to life*
5. *You believe in yourself*

Realization is where you start saying good bye to the old baggage. It is the point in your mind where it is time to let go of the old and embrace the new.

Take this time meditate on the wonderful opportunities you are about to have. As a matter of fact start to see yourself in your Powerful Transformation……Visualize your new reality…See you next week

Say "Goodbye to the Old Baggage"

Tip #6 – Visualize

Tip #6: *The sixth tip for getting a C.L.E.A.R.* ***V****.I.E.W.* ™ *is to* **visualize** *your Powerful transformation.*

Think about some of the most successful people that you know, whether it be the Creators of your favorite movie, CEO's of Fortune 500 companies, Leaders of flourishing Worship centers, or the inventor of the World Wide Web all of them have one thing in common. At some point they had a vision for the success that they have today.

This sixth tip is the most important tip of them all, because from your vision the very existence of your Powerful Transformation will be born.

How many times have you been sitting in a still place, and just started drifting off in a day dream? Your mind goes from what you need to do the remainder of the day, to what you need to do at work, to something one of your friends said to something else then you knap yourself of it. For your Powerful transformation I want you to do what I call a "Vision Dream"

A vision dream is when you intentionally take time to day dream with the purpose of forming a mental image of the transformation that you are trying to achieve.

For example if your Powerful transformation is to advance in your career by competing for a promotion, then one of your vision dream sessions would start out by you realizing that have the ability to get the job (Tip #5—realize) Ok at this point you would need to visual what really having the job would look like. You may need some additional training on computers software, you may need to gain more knowledge in the field of expertise for the position, you may need to form relationships with the people in the organization or you may need to update your wardrobe. Whatever the transformation is to allow you to succeed in the transformation, you need to allow yourself to dream about it. You need to allow yourself to see it in your mind.

Just like a day dream a vision dream transports you to the state of seeing yourself in the transformation, but how a vision dream is different is that a vision dream is not a fantasy or a memory, it is a conscious thought process of visualizing your reality for your transformation.

To have an effective vision dream session do the following:
1. *Plan time 20 to 30 minutes alone –get away from kids, the husband, the dog, the friends*
2. *Get a note book—it is important that you capture your vision*
3. *Relax*
4. *Ask three questions that you want answered and let your mind and spirit give you the answers*
5. *Capture them in the note book*
6. *After your time is up review your notes and then you are ready to move to the next Tip*

I could spend days talking about your vision, vision dreams, vision statements, being a visionary, and being a visionary leader because all of these things are hats you will wear. You do not just have one vision; once you have achieve the first level of transformation that you initially were able to receive then you open the door to go to a higher level of Powerful transformation.

Sweet dreams…vision dreams that is…See you next week

Sweet dreams… vision dreams that is

Tip #7 – Initiate

*Tip #7: The seventh tip for getting a C.L.E.A.R. V.**I**.E.W. ™ is to **initiate** the vision for your Powerful transformation.*

Wouda Shoulda Coulda...how many times have you heard that or even said that yourself? I was reading a magazine and saw a little cartoon where there was a cat laying on a Psychologist lounge. He looked at her and said "I just feel I should have accomplished more with nine lives". Unlike the cat we only get one life and this is your opportunity to stop wondering about what could be; it is time to take action and make your ONE life the best life you can have RIGHT NOW.

You are now to the point where you can start making things happen for yourself. Now that you have had a vision dream or two, you are ready to initiate the transformation that you have been working on.

Everybody, Somebody, Anybody and Nobody

This is a little story about four people named Everybody, Somebody, Anybody and Nobody

There was an important job that needed to be initiated and Everybody was sure that Somebody would do it.

Anybody could have done it, but Nobody did it

Somebody got angry about that because it was Everybody's job!!

Everybody thought that Anybody could do it, but Nobody realized that Everybody would not do it.

It ended up that Everybody blamed Somebody when Nobody did what Anybody could have done.

Author Unknown.

In your life you do not have Everybody, Somebody, Anybody and Nobody to count on to initiate the plans and steps you need to take to experience your Powerful Transformations, you only have you! To initiate something means that you take action to start a process. A transformation is to take action to change your situation from what it once was. This week is the week you cause your transformation to start to materialize. Up to this point the transformation has been designed to take root in your mind. You have meditated on being committed to your transformation, you have taken time to research and increase your knowledge about your transformation, you have mustard up the energy to stay engaged in your transformation, you have created your mantra and articulated your transformation over and over which has allowed it to connect with your spirit, you have made your transformation real by believing that YOU can make this powerful transformation come to past, you visualized yourself walking, living and being in your Powerful transformation....Now it is the action of manifestation in your physical and tangible transformation, the initiation of the transformation.

Following these 5 simple steps will help you initiate the vision for your Powerful transformation

1. Select a date to put the vision into action

2. Put the right people or things into place to ensure that the initiation flows smoothly

3. Have a back up in place—If you need a pair of tennis shoes (take two), If you need 5 table clothes take 8. If you are supposed to be there at 4 get there at 3.

4. Be mentally ready

5. GO!!!

In the last tip I used getting a promotion as an example. I am going to draw from that same example for initiation. Ok one of the visions I mentioned was that you may identify your need to learn computer software to be competitive for your next promotion. Now that you have visualized this and learned what training you need, where to get it from ((Tip #2), you are now ready to initiate the vision by paying for the training and walking into the class room. Look around Your transformation is now your life. It's this Exciting?

Make your life the best life you can have RIGHT NOW.

Tip #8 – Evaluate

Tip #8: *The eighth tip for getting a C.L.E.A.R. V.I.**E**.W. ™ is to **evaluate** your progress once you have initiated your Powerful transformation.*

Arrhhh What? A test? I don't want to be tested; I don't want to be judged. I don't want to know if I failed. Listen my friends there is no failing in a Powerful transformation so do not even try that.

Anytime you make changes in your life you have to assess what you have done to see if the change is working like you planned; to see if you are getting the results that you hoped for.

I find that people will often quit initiating their vision if they see any sign of what they think is failure. Most times it is not a failure the transformation just needed to be reset and redirected. If you do not evaluate what changes need to be made then you will allow yourself to get stuck and revert back to the life style that makes you unhappy and unfulfilled.

Being able to evaluate the transformation and realign the vision is the main key to discovering your secret receipt.

You have already written down the Powerful transformation that you would like to achieve and have initiated a step or two to get the transformation going. Now you should be able to evaluate if the actions you initiated are working.

These four evaluation steps will help you check to see where you are

1. *Begin by reviewing the vision that you initiated.*

    For example, if your vision was to lose 1 lb in a week by eating 100 less per day and exercising for 30 minutes per day then you would go back and review your Journal to see if you stuck to the plan. If the process allowed you to receive the results you envisioned then Your Powerful transformation was reached

2. *Compare what was to what is now.*

    Even if you see a change in a small area it is worth sticking to the transformation.

3. *Make any necessary adjustments.*

    If you see that you need to make adjustments do that as well—go back to Tip 6

4. *Enjoy the victory of achieving your Powerful Transformation*

The evaluation process allows you to make adjustments to the vision. It is just important as the initiation. You are almost there don't stop now…See you next week!!!

If you see that you need to make adjustments do that, but don't ever give up!

Tips #9 – WIN!

Tip #9: *The ninth tip for getting a C.L.E.A.R. V.I.E.* ***W***. ™ *is to celebrate your BIG* **WIN**!! *You have achieved the Powerful Transformation that you set out to accomplish.*
DO You know that you are a Winner? You were created to triumph, to overcome, to be the victor and the champion. When it comes to being powerful, no one can transform you like you. Why because everyone has a different definition of success so what may look like a loss to you is a win to somebody else and vise versa.

When you have completed all the tips to accomplish the powerful transformation, be sure to celebrate the Win by

1. Saying," I made it, I had MY Powerful transformation in _____ "
2. Make the celebration about YOU!
3. Reward yourself with something that you like

Winning in your Powerful transformation shows that you can make a commitment to yourself, learn how to accomplish the dream, get energized to carry out your plan, articulate what you want to accomplish, realize that your dream is tangible, visualize the process to get where you want to be, imitate the transformation steps, evaluate your progress and make adjustments if needed then celebrate your BIG WIN!!!

Now that you have a C.L.E.A.R. V.I.E.W. ™

Wasn't this a wonderful journey? Now that you have a C.L.E.A.R. V.I.E.W. ™ please use them to continue to make Powerful transformations in your life. There are no limits to abundance you can enjoy in your life through following these tips. A C.L.E.A.R. V.I.E.W. ™ is all you need. I hope you have enjoyed reading these Tips as much as I have enjoyed sharing them with you. They have worked for me for many years. I am glad to be able to pass my blessing on to you.

Reference

John Cena & Phrase "You can't see me" , Rey Mysterio & Rick Flare and All WWE programming, talent names, images, likenesses, slogans, wrestling moves, trademarks, logos and copyrights are the exclusive property of WWE, Inc. and its subsidiaries. There is no relationship between the WWE and Tabitha McClarity Coaching & Consulting, LLC information was used for educational purposes only. All Right Reserved by WWE. For more information about wrestling please visit http://www.wwe.com/

About the Author

Inspirational, Empowering, and Innovative are just a few words to describe Tabitha's personally. Tabitha captivates her audiences and clients with a freshness and realness that is unmatched.

Her background includes experience over the last 20 plus years moving from working on the production line to working in Human Resources, to Employee Relations then to Training and development in a food manufacturing Company. Upon completing her undergraduate degree (as a single mother of four0 she changed careers and gained experience at a Fortune 500 Utility company in a Covered (Union) position and was again consistently promoted into various positions including Controller, Compliance Comptroller & Financial Team Leader.

Tabitha had always had the Entrepreneur Spirit and in 2004 while in the last few months of completing her Master's in Business Administration, took a leap of faith and started her first business – Jay Pearl Tax & Financial Services, LLC located in Rockmart GA. Still working Full-time and preparing taxes part-time, Tabitha was able to complete 72 returns her first year and over the last seven years continued to work full-time, raise a family and prepare Taxes part-time. In that same year Tabitha answered the call from God and began to preach the Gospel under the leadership of Pastor Ramon Arnold

Throughout her life Tabitha has always been an encourager and cheerleader and often used her blessings to encourage others to accomplish whatever they dreamed. She found that most of the times during Tax season people wanted to talk to her and would often ask, "What were her Keys to Success?" Or they would talk to her about career issues, relationship issues etc. As a continuous learner Tabitha had taken all of her successes and failures and was able to articulate it in a way others understood.

In 2010 after hearing some dynamic motivational speakers Tabitha realized that she had been doing this almost all of her life. She desired to see people operate in the success that life had for them. She understood that sometimes the past could cloud a person's vision and began to put together information from questions she had gotten from her clients. In 2011 Tabitha McClarity Coaching and Consulting was born.

Since that time Tabitha has been the Key note speaker at Women's programs and Government Agency Family First Programs. She has also conducted Financial Education programs for the Youth and developed an Entrepreneurial Spirit Seminar for new to experience Business owners.

She invites you to take control of your life, don't let anything or anyone stop you…YOUR POWERFUL TRANSFORMATION is in the palms of your hands…..

Please look for these Titles by Tabitha L. McClarity

I Forgive Me: 31 days of Self Forgiveness:
In order to be able to TRULY forgive others I have to forgive me first!!!

Empowerment...My Power...ME:
5 Steps to creating Self Encouragement, Self Respect and Self Power

ITeam: I Don't Care What Anyone Says...There is an "I" in Team!!!

No Money Mo Problems: 6 Steps to Reduce Debt and Live With the Money You Make

R-E-S-P-E-C-T the Money and it will stay with you longer

Three Tenths Money Strategy: Savings, Tithing and Investing my way Financial Freedom

Lord I want to be made whole: Spiritually, Mentally, Physically & Financially; The four stages to experience true Wholeness (four book series)

For more information about this Author, Speaker, Life/Success Coach visit us on the web ***www.tabithamcclarity.com***

www.ingramcontent.com/pod-product-compliance
Lightning Source LLC
Chambersburg PA
CBHW031437040426
42444CB00006B/856